Welcome

We're So Happy You're Here!

Please sign our

Guest Book

&

share your experience with us
and future guests.

Guest Name/s: _____

Dates of my/our visit: _____ To _____   I/we traveled from: _____

Reason for my/our trip: _____

Message to the host: _____

_____

_____

Favorite Moments / Special Highlights Of My/Our Stay

_____

_____

_____

_____

Places I/We Recommend (Restaurants - Entertainment — Must See Sites)

_____

_____

_____

_____

Guest Name/s: _____

Dates of my/our visit: _____ To _____ I/we traveled from: _____

Reason for my/our trip: _____

Message to the host: _____

_____

_____

Favorite Moments / Special Highlights Of My/Our Stay

_____

_____

_____

_____

Places I/We Recommend (Restaurants - Entertainment – Must See Sites)

_____

_____

_____

_____

Guest Name/s: _____

Dates of my/our visit: _____ To _____ I/we traveled from: _____

Reason for my/our trip: _____

Message to the host: _____

_____

_____

Favorite Moments / Special Highlights Of My/Our Stay

_____

_____

_____

_____

Places I/We Recommend (Restaurants - Entertainment — Must See Sites)

_____

_____

_____

_____

Guest Name/s: _____

Dates of my/our visit: _____ To _____ I/we traveled from: _____

Reason for my/our trip: _____

Message to the host: _____

_____

_____

Favorite Moments / Special Highlights Of My/Our Stay

_____

_____

_____

_____

Places I/We Recommend (Restaurants - Entertainment — Must See Sites)

_____

_____

_____

_____

Guest Name/s: _____

Dates of my/our visit: _____ To _____ I/we traveled from: _____

Reason for my/our trip: _____

Message to the host: _____

_____

_____

Favorite Moments / Special Highlights Of My/Our Stay

_____

_____

_____

_____

Places I/We Recommend (Restaurants - Entertainment — Must See Sites)

_____

_____

_____

_____

Guest Name/s: _____

Dates of my/our visit: _____ To _____ I/we traveled from: _____

Reason for my/our trip: _____

Message to the host: _____

_____

_____

Favorite Moments / Special Highlights Of My/Our Stay

_____

_____

_____

_____

Places I/We Recommend (Restaurants - Entertainment — Must See Sites)

_____

_____

_____

_____

Guest Name/s: _____

Dates of my/our visit: _____ To _____ I/we traveled from: _____

Reason for my/our trip: _____

Message to the host: _____
_____
_____

Favorite Moments / Special Highlights Of My/Our Stay

_____
_____
_____
_____

Places I/We Recommend (Restaurants - Entertainment – Must See Sites)

_____
_____
_____
_____

Guest Name/s: _____

Dates of my/our visit: _____ To _____ I/we traveled from: _____

Reason for my/our trip: _____

Message to the host: _____

_____

_____

Favorite Moments / Special Highlights Of My/Our Stay

_____

_____

_____

_____

Places I/We Recommend (Restaurants - Entertainment — Must See Sites)

_____

_____

_____

_____

Guest Name/s: _____

Dates of my/our visit: _____ To _____ I/we traveled from: _____

Reason for my/our trip: _____

Message to the host: _____
_____
_____

Favorite Moments / Special Highlights Of My/Our Stay

_____
_____
_____
_____

Places I/We Recommend (Restaurants - Entertainment — Must See Sites)

_____
_____
_____
_____

Guest Name/s: _____

Dates of my/our visit: _____ To _____ I/we traveled from: _____

Reason for my/our trip: _____

Message to the host: _____

_____

_____

Favorite Moments / Special Highlights Of My/Our Stay

_____

_____

_____

_____

Places I/We Recommend (Restaurants - Entertainment — Must See Sites)

_____

_____

_____

_____

Guest Name/s: _____

Dates of my/our visit: _____ To _____ I/we traveled from: _____

Reason for my/our trip: _____

Message to the host: _____

_____

_____

Favorite Moments / Special Highlights Of My/Our Stay

_____

_____

_____

_____

Places I/We Recommend (Restaurants - Entertainment — Must See Sites)

_____

_____

_____

_____

Guest Name/s: _____

Dates of my/our visit: _____ To _____ I/we traveled from: _____

Reason for my/our trip: _____

Message to the host: _____
_____
_____

Favorite Moments / Special Highlights Of My/Our Stay

_____
_____
_____
_____

Places I/We Recommend (Restaurants - Entertainment — Must See Sites)

_____
_____
_____
_____

Guest Name/s: _____

Dates of my/our visit: _____ To _____ I/we traveled from: _____

Reason for my/our trip: _____

Message to the host: _____
_____
_____

Favorite Moments / Special Highlights Of My/Our Stay

_____
_____
_____
_____

Places I/We Recommend (Restaurants - Entertainment – Must See Sites)

_____
_____
_____
_____

Guest Name/s: _____

Dates of my/our visit: _____ To _____ I/we traveled from: _____

Reason for my/our trip: _____

Message to the host: _____

_____

_____

Favorite Moments / Special Highlights Of My/Our Stay

_____

_____

_____

_____

Places I/We Recommend (Restaurants - Entertainment — Must See Sites)

_____

_____

_____

_____

Guest Name/s: _____

Dates of my/our visit: _____ To _____   I/we traveled from: _____

Reason for my/our trip: _____

Message to the host: _____
_____
_____

Favorite Moments / Special Highlights Of My/Our Stay

_____
_____
_____
_____

Places I/We Recommend (Restaurants - Entertainment – Must See Sites)

_____
_____
_____
_____

Guest Name/s: _____

Dates of my/our visit: _____ To _____   I/we traveled from: _____

Reason for my/our trip: _____

Message to the host: _____
_____
_____

Favorite Moments / Special Highlights Of My/Our Stay

_____
_____
_____
_____

Places I/We Recommend (Restaurants - Entertainment — Must See Sites)

_____
_____
_____
_____

Guest Name/s: _____

Dates of my/our visit: _____ To _____   I/we traveled from: _____

Reason for my/our trip: _____

Message to the host: _____
_____
_____

Favorite Moments / Special Highlights Of My/Our Stay

_____
_____
_____
_____

Places I/We Recommend (Restaurants - Entertainment – Must See Sites)

_____
_____
_____
_____

Guest Name/s: _____

Dates of my/our visit: _____ To _____   I/we traveled from: _____

Reason for my/our trip: _____

Message to the host: _____
_____
_____

Favorite Moments / Special Highlights Of My/Our Stay

_____
_____
_____
_____

Places I/We Recommend (Restaurants - Entertainment – Must See Sites)

_____
_____
_____
_____

Guest Name/s: _____

Dates of my/our visit: _____ To _____ I/we traveled from: _____

Reason for my/our trip: _____

Message to the host: _____

_____

_____

Favorite Moments / Special Highlights Of My/Our Stay

_____

_____

_____

_____

Places I/We Recommend (Restaurants - Entertainment — Must See Sites)

_____

_____

_____

_____

Guest Name/s: _____

Dates of my/our visit: _____ To _____ I/we traveled from: _____

Reason for my/our trip: _____

Message to the host: _____
_____
_____

Favorite Moments / Special Highlights Of My/Our Stay

_____
_____
_____
_____

Places I/We Recommend (Restaurants - Entertainment — Must See Sites)

_____
_____
_____
_____

Guest Name/s: _____

Dates of my/our visit: _____ To _____ I/we traveled from: _____

Reason for my/our trip: _____

Message to the host: _____

_____

_____

Favorite Moments / Special Highlights Of My/Our Stay

_____

_____

_____

_____

Places I/We Recommend (Restaurants - Entertainment — Must See Sites)

_____

_____

_____

_____

Guest Name/s: _____

Dates of my/our visit: _____ To _____ I/we traveled from: _____

Reason for my/our trip: _____

Message to the host: _____
_____
_____

Favorite Moments / Special Highlights Of My/Our Stay

_____
_____
_____
_____

Places I/We Recommend (Restaurants - Entertainment — Must See Sites)

_____
_____
_____
_____

Guest Name/s: _____

Dates of my/our visit: _____ To _____ I/we traveled from: _____

Reason for my/our trip: _____

Message to the host: _____

_____

_____

Favorite Moments / Special Highlights Of My/Our Stay

_____

_____

_____

_____

Places I/We Recommend (Restaurants - Entertainment — Must See Sites)

_____

_____

_____

_____

Guest Name/s: _____

Dates of my/our visit: _____ To _____ I/we traveled from: _____

Reason for my/our trip: _____

Message to the host: _____

_____

_____

Favorite Moments / Special Highlights Of My/Our Stay

_____

_____

_____

_____

Places I/We Recommend (Restaurants - Entertainment – Must See Sites)

_____

_____

_____

_____

Guest Name/s: _____

Dates of my/our visit: _____ To _____ I/we traveled from: _____

Reason for my/our trip: _____

Message to the host: _____

_____

_____

Favorite Moments / Special Highlights Of My/Our Stay

_____

_____

_____

_____

Places I/We Recommend (Restaurants - Entertainment – Must See Sites)

_____

_____

_____

_____

Guest Name/s: _____

Dates of my/our visit: _____ To _____ I/we traveled from: _____

Reason for my/our trip: _____

Message to the host: _____
_____
_____

Favorite Moments / Special Highlights Of My/Our Stay

_____
_____
_____
_____

Places I/We Recommend (Restaurants - Entertainment — Must See Sites)

_____
_____
_____
_____

Guest Name/s: _____

Dates of my/our visit: _____ To _____ I/we traveled from: _____

Reason for my/our trip: _____

Message to the host: _____

_____

_____

Favorite Moments / Special Highlights Of My/Our Stay

_____

_____

_____

_____

Places I/We Recommend (Restaurants - Entertainment — Must See Sites)

_____

_____

_____

_____

Guest Name/s: _____

Dates of my/our visit: _____ To _____ I/we traveled from: _____

Reason for my/our trip: _____

Message to the host: _____
_____
_____

Favorite Moments / Special Highlights Of My/Our Stay

_____
_____
_____
_____

Places I/We Recommend (Restaurants - Entertainment — Must See Sites)

_____
_____
_____
_____

Guest Name/s: _____

Dates of my/our visit: _____ To _____ I/we traveled from: _____

Reason for my/our trip: _____

Message to the host: _____

_____

_____

Favorite Moments / Special Highlights Of My/Our Stay

_____

_____

_____

_____

Places I/We Recommend (Restaurants - Entertainment – Must See Sites)

_____

_____

_____

_____

Guest Name/s: _____

Dates of my/our visit: _____ To _____ I/we traveled from: _____

Reason for my/our trip: _____

Message to the host: _____

_____

_____

Favorite Moments / Special Highlights Of My/Our Stay

_____

_____

_____

_____

Places I/We Recommend (Restaurants - Entertainment — Must See Sites)

_____

_____

_____

_____

Guest Name/s: _____

Dates of my/our visit: _____ To _____   I/we traveled from: _____

Reason for my/our trip: _____

Message to the host: _____

_____

_____

Favorite Moments / Special Highlights Of My/Our Stay

_____

_____

_____

_____

Places I/We Recommend (Restaurants - Entertainment — Must See Sites)

_____

_____

_____

_____

Guest Name/s: _____

Dates of my/our visit: _____ To _____ I/we traveled from: _____

Reason for my/our trip: _____

Message to the host: _____
_____
_____

Favorite Moments / Special Highlights Of My/Our Stay

_____
_____
_____
_____

Places I/We Recommend (Restaurants - Entertainment — Must See Sites)

_____
_____
_____
_____

Guest Name/s: _____

Dates of my/our visit: _____ To _____ I/we traveled from: _____

Reason for my/our trip: _____

Message to the host: _____
_____
_____

Favorite Moments / Special Highlights Of My/Our Stay

_____
_____
_____
_____

Places I/We Recommend (Restaurants - Entertainment – Must See Sites)

_____
_____
_____
_____

Guest Name/s: _____

Dates of my/our visit: _____ To _____ I/we traveled from: _____

Reason for my/our trip: _____

Message to the host: _____

_____

_____

Favorite Moments / Special Highlights Of My/Our Stay

_____

_____

_____

_____

Places I/We Recommend (Restaurants - Entertainment – Must See Sites)

_____

_____

_____

_____

Guest Name/s: _____

Dates of my/our visit: _____ To _____ I/we traveled from: _____

Reason for my/our trip: _____

Message to the host: _____

_____

_____

Favorite Moments / Special Highlights Of My/Our Stay

_____

_____

_____

_____

Places I/We Recommend (Restaurants - Entertainment — Must See Sites)

_____

_____

_____

_____

Guest Name/s: _____

Dates of my/our visit: _____ To _____ I/we traveled from: _____

Reason for my/our trip: _____

Message to the host: _____
_____
_____

Favorite Moments / Special Highlights Of My/Our Stay

_____
_____
_____
_____

Places I/We Recommend (Restaurants - Entertainment – Must See Sites)

_____
_____
_____
_____

Guest Name/s: _____

Dates of my/our visit: _____ To _____ I/we traveled from: _____

Reason for my/our trip: _____

Message to the host: _____

_____

_____

Favorite Moments / Special Highlights Of My/Our Stay

_____

_____

_____

_____

Places I/We Recommend (Restaurants - Entertainment — Must See Sites)

_____

_____

_____

_____

Guest Name/s: _____

Dates of my/our visit: _____ To _____ I/we traveled from: _____

Reason for my/our trip: _____

Message to the host: _____
_____
_____

Favorite Moments / Special Highlights Of My/Our Stay

_____
_____
_____
_____

Places I/We Recommend (Restaurants - Entertainment — Must See Sites)

_____
_____
_____
_____

Guest Name/s: _____

Dates of my/our visit: _____ To _____ I/we traveled from: _____

Reason for my/our trip: _____

Message to the host: _____

_____

_____

Favorite Moments / Special Highlights Of My/Our Stay

_____

_____

_____

_____

Places I/We Recommend (Restaurants - Entertainment — Must See Sites)

_____

_____

_____

_____

Guest Name/s: _____

Dates of my/our visit: _____ To _____ I/we traveled from: _____

Reason for my/our trip: _____

Message to the host: _____

_____

_____

Favorite Moments / Special Highlights Of My/Our Stay

_____

_____

_____

_____

Places I/We Recommend (Restaurants - Entertainment — Must See Sites)

_____

_____

_____

_____

Guest Name/s: _____

Dates of my/our visit: _____ To _____ I/we traveled from: _____

Reason for my/our trip: _____

Message to the host: _____

_____

_____

Favorite Moments / Special Highlights Of My/Our Stay

_____

_____

_____

_____

Places I/We Recommend (Restaurants - Entertainment — Must See Sites)

_____

_____

_____

_____

Guest Name/s: _____

Dates of my/our visit: _____ To _____   I/we traveled from: _____

Reason for my/our trip: _____

Message to the host: _____

_____

_____

Favorite Moments / Special Highlights Of My/Our Stay

_____

_____

_____

_____

Places I/We Recommend (Restaurants - Entertainment — Must See Sites)

_____

_____

_____

_____

Guest Name/s: _____

Dates of my/our visit: _____ To _____ I/we traveled from: _____

Reason for my/our trip: _____

Message to the host: _____

_____

_____

Favorite Moments / Special Highlights Of My/Our Stay

_____

_____

_____

_____

Places I/We Recommend (Restaurants - Entertainment — Must See Sites)

_____

_____

_____

_____

Guest Name/s: _____

Dates of my/our visit: _____ To _____ I/we traveled from: _____

Reason for my/our trip: _____

Message to the host: _____
_____
_____
_____

Favorite Moments / Special Highlights Of My/Our Stay

_____
_____
_____
_____

Places I/We Recommend (Restaurants - Entertainment — Must See Sites)

_____
_____
_____
_____

Guest Name/s: _____

Dates of my/our visit: _____ To _____ I/we traveled from: _____

Reason for my/our trip: _____

Message to the host: _____

_____

_____

Favorite Moments / Special Highlights Of My/Our Stay

_____

_____

_____

_____

Places I/We Recommend (Restaurants - Entertainment — Must See Sites)

_____

_____

_____

_____

Guest Name/s: _____

Dates of my/our visit: _____ To _____ I/we traveled from: _____

Reason for my/our trip: _____

Message to the host: _____

_____

_____

Favorite Moments / Special Highlights Of My/Our Stay

_____

_____

_____

_____

Places I/We Recommend (Restaurants - Entertainment — Must See Sites)

_____

_____

_____

_____

Guest Name/s: _____

Dates of my/our visit: _____ To _____ I/we traveled from: _____

Reason for my/our trip: _____

Message to the host: _____

_____

_____

Favorite Moments / Special Highlights Of My/Our Stay

_____

_____

_____

_____

Places I/We Recommend (Restaurants - Entertainment — Must See Sites)

_____

_____

_____

_____

Guest Name/s: _____

Dates of my/our visit: _____ To _____ I/we traveled from: _____

Reason for my/our trip: _____

⟵⟶

Message to the host: _____
_____
_____

⟵⟶

Favorite Moments / Special Highlights Of My/Our Stay

_____
_____
_____
_____

⟵⟶

Places I/We Recommend (Restaurants - Entertainment – Must See Sites)

_____
_____
_____
_____

Guest Name/s: _____

Dates of my/our visit: _____ To _____ I/we traveled from: _____

Reason for my/our trip: _____

Message to the host: _____

_____

_____

Favorite Moments / Special Highlights Of My/Our Stay

_____

_____

_____

_____

Places I/We Recommend (Restaurants - Entertainment — Must See Sites)

_____

_____

_____

_____

Guest Name/s: _____

Dates of my/our visit: _____ To _____ I/we traveled from: _____

Reason for my/our trip: _____

Message to the host: _____

_____

_____

Favorite Moments / Special Highlights Of My/Our Stay

_____

_____

_____

_____

Places I/We Recommend (Restaurants - Entertainment — Must See Sites)

_____

_____

_____

_____

Guest Name/s: _____

Dates of my/our visit: _____ To _____ I/we traveled from: _____

Reason for my/our trip: _____

Message to the host: _____

_____

_____

Favorite Moments / Special Highlights Of My/Our Stay

_____

_____

_____

_____

Places I/We Recommend (Restaurants - Entertainment – Must See Sites)

_____

_____

_____

_____

Guest Name/s: _____

Dates of my/our visit: _____ To _____   I/we traveled from: _____

Reason for my/our trip: _____

Message to the host: _____
_____
_____

Favorite Moments / Special Highlights Of My/Our Stay

_____
_____
_____
_____

Places I/We Recommend (Restaurants - Entertainment — Must See Sites)

_____
_____
_____
_____

Guest Name/s: _____

Dates of my/our visit: _____ To _____ I/we traveled from: _____

Reason for my/our trip: _____

Message to the host: _____

_____

_____

Favorite Moments / Special Highlights Of My/Our Stay

_____

_____

_____

_____

Places I/We Recommend (Restaurants - Entertainment — Must See Sites)

_____

_____

_____

_____

Guest Name/s: _____

Dates of my/our visit: _____ To _____ I/we traveled from: _____

Reason for my/our trip: _____

Message to the host: _____

_____

_____

Favorite Moments / Special Highlights Of My/Our Stay

_____

_____

_____

_____

Places I/We Recommend (Restaurants - Entertainment — Must See Sites)

_____

_____

_____

_____

Guest Name/s: _____

Dates of my/our visit: _____ To _____ I/we traveled from: _____

Reason for my/our trip: _____

Message to the host: _____
_____
_____

Favorite Moments / Special Highlights Of My/Our Stay
_____
_____
_____
_____

Places I/We Recommend (Restaurants - Entertainment — Must See Sites)
_____
_____
_____
_____

Guest Name/s: _____

Dates of my/our visit: _____ To _____   I/we traveled from: _____

Reason for my/our trip: _____

Message to the host: _____
_____
_____

Favorite Moments / Special Highlights Of My/Our Stay

_____
_____
_____
_____

Places I/We Recommend (Restaurants - Entertainment — Must See Sites)

_____
_____
_____
_____

Guest Name/s: _____

Dates of my/our visit: _____ To _____ I/we traveled from: _____

Reason for my/our trip: _____

Message to the host: _____

_____

_____

Favorite Moments / Special Highlights Of My/Our Stay

_____

_____

_____

_____

Places I/We Recommend (Restaurants - Entertainment — Must See Sites)

_____

_____

_____

_____

Guest Name/s: _____

Dates of my/our visit: _____ To _____ I/we traveled from: _____

Reason for my/our trip: _____

Message to the host: _____

_____

_____

Favorite Moments / Special Highlights Of My/Our Stay

_____

_____

_____

_____

Places I/We Recommend (Restaurants - Entertainment — Must See Sites)

_____

_____

_____

_____

Guest Name/s: _____

Dates of my/our visit: _____ To _____ I/we traveled from: _____

Reason for my/our trip: _____

Message to the host: _____

_____

_____

Favorite Moments / Special Highlights Of My/Our Stay

_____

_____

_____

_____

Places I/We Recommend (Restaurants - Entertainment — Must See Sites)

_____

_____

_____

_____

Guest Name/s: _____

Dates of my/our visit: _____ To _____ I/we traveled from: _____

Reason for my/our trip: _____

Message to the host: _____
_____
_____

Favorite Moments / Special Highlights Of My/Our Stay

_____
_____
_____
_____

Places I/We Recommend (Restaurants - Entertainment — Must See Sites)

_____
_____
_____
_____

Guest Name/s: _____

Dates of my/our visit: _____ To _____   I/we traveled from: _____

Reason for my/our trip: _____

Message to the host: _____

_____

_____

Favorite Moments / Special Highlights Of My/Our Stay

_____

_____

_____

_____

Places I/We Recommend (Restaurants - Entertainment – Must See Sites)

_____

_____

_____

_____

Guest Name/s: _____

Dates of my/our visit: _____ To _____ I/we traveled from: _____

Reason for my/our trip: _____

Message to the host: _____

_____

_____

Favorite Moments / Special Highlights Of My/Our Stay

_____

_____

_____

_____

Places I/We Recommend (Restaurants - Entertainment — Must See Sites)

_____

_____

_____

_____

Guest Name/s: _____

Dates of my/our visit: _____ To _____ I/we traveled from: _____

Reason for my/our trip: _____

Message to the host: _____

_____

_____

Favorite Moments / Special Highlights Of My/Our Stay

_____

_____

_____

_____

Places I/We Recommend (Restaurants - Entertainment — Must See Sites)

_____

_____

_____

_____

Guest Name/s: _____

Dates of my/our visit: _____ To _____ I/we traveled from: _____

Reason for my/our trip: _____

Message to the host: _____
_____
_____

Favorite Moments / Special Highlights Of My/Our Stay

_____
_____
_____
_____

Places I/We Recommend (Restaurants - Entertainment — Must See Sites)

_____
_____
_____
_____

Guest Name/s: _____

Dates of my/our visit: _____ To _____ I/we traveled from: _____

Reason for my/our trip: _____

Message to the host: _____

_____

_____

Favorite Moments / Special Highlights Of My/Our Stay

_____

_____

_____

_____

Places I/We Recommend (Restaurants - Entertainment — Must See Sites)

_____

_____

_____

_____

Guest Name/s: _____

Dates of my/our visit: _____ To _____ I/we traveled from: _____

Reason for my/our trip: _____

Message to the host: _____

_____

_____

Favorite Moments / Special Highlights Of My/Our Stay

_____

_____

_____

_____

Places I/We Recommend (Restaurants - Entertainment — Must See Sites)

_____

_____

_____

_____

Guest Name/s: _____

Dates of my/our visit: _____ To _____ I/we traveled from: _____

Reason for my/our trip: _____

Message to the host: _____

_____

_____

Favorite Moments / Special Highlights Of My/Our Stay

_____

_____

_____

_____

Places I/We Recommend (Restaurants - Entertainment — Must See Sites)

_____

_____

_____

_____

Guest Name/s: _____

Dates of my/our visit: _____ To _____ I/we traveled from: _____

Reason for my/our trip: _____

Message to the host: _____

_____

_____

Favorite Moments / Special Highlights Of My/Our Stay

_____

_____

_____

_____

Places I/We Recommend (Restaurants - Entertainment — Must See Sites)

_____

_____

_____

_____

Guest Name/s: _____

Dates of my/our visit: _____ To _____ I/we traveled from: _____

Reason for my/our trip: _____

Message to the host: _____

_____

_____

Favorite Moments / Special Highlights Of My/Our Stay

_____

_____

_____

_____

Places I/We Recommend (Restaurants - Entertainment — Must See Sites)

_____

_____

_____

_____

Guest Name/s: _____

Dates of my/our visit: _____ To _____ I/we traveled from: _____

Reason for my/our trip: _____

Message to the host: _____
_____
_____

Favorite Moments / Special Highlights Of My/Our Stay

_____
_____
_____
_____

Places I/We Recommend (Restaurants - Entertainment – Must See Sites)

_____
_____
_____
_____

Guest Name/s: _____

Dates of my/our visit: _____ To _____ I/we traveled from: _____

Reason for my/our trip: _____

Message to the host: _____
_____
_____

Favorite Moments / Special Highlights Of My/Our Stay

_____
_____
_____
_____

Places I/We Recommend (Restaurants - Entertainment — Must See Sites)

_____
_____
_____
_____

Guest Name/s: _____

Dates of my/our visit: _____ To _____ I/we traveled from: _____

Reason for my/our trip: _____

Message to the host: _____
_____
_____

Favorite Moments / Special Highlights Of My/Our Stay

_____
_____
_____
_____

Places I/We Recommend (Restaurants - Entertainment — Must See Sites)

_____
_____
_____
_____

Guest Name/s: _____

Dates of my/our visit: _____ To _____ I/we traveled from: _____

Reason for my/our trip: _____

Message to the host: _____

_____

_____

Favorite Moments / Special Highlights Of My/Our Stay

_____

_____

_____

_____

Places I/We Recommend (Restaurants - Entertainment — Must See Sites)

_____

_____

_____

_____

Guest Name/s: _____

Dates of my/our visit: _____ To _____ I/we traveled from: _____

Reason for my/our trip: _____

Message to the host: _____
_____
_____

Favorite Moments / Special Highlights Of My/Our Stay

_____
_____
_____
_____

Places I/We Recommend (Restaurants - Entertainment — Must See Sites)

_____
_____
_____
_____

Guest Name/s: _____

Dates of my/our visit: _____ To _____ I/we traveled from: _____

Reason for my/our trip: _____

Message to the host: _____

_____

_____

Favorite Moments / Special Highlights Of My/Our Stay

_____

_____

_____

_____

Places I/We Recommend (Restaurants - Entertainment — Must See Sites)

_____

_____

_____

_____

Guest Name/s: _____

Dates of my/our visit: _____ To _____ I/we traveled from: _____

Reason for my/our trip: _____

Message to the host: _____

_____

_____

Favorite Moments / Special Highlights Of My/Our Stay

_____

_____

_____

_____

Places I/We Recommend (Restaurants - Entertainment — Must See Sites)

_____

_____

_____

_____

Guest Name/s: _____

Dates of my/our visit: _____ To _____ I/we traveled from: _____

Reason for my/our trip: _____

Message to the host: _____

_____

_____

Favorite Moments / Special Highlights Of My/Our Stay

_____

_____

_____

_____

Places I/We Recommend (Restaurants - Entertainment — Must See Sites)

_____

_____

_____

_____

Guest Name/s: _____

Dates of my/our visit: _____ To _____ I/we traveled from: _____

Reason for my/our trip: _____

Message to the host: _____

_____

_____

Favorite Moments / Special Highlights Of My/Our Stay

_____

_____

_____

_____

Places I/We Recommend (Restaurants - Entertainment — Must See Sites)

_____

_____

_____

_____

Guest Name/s: _____

Dates of my/our visit: _____ To _____   I/we traveled from: _____

Reason for my/our trip: _____

Message to the host: _____

_____

_____

Favorite Moments / Special Highlights Of My/Our Stay

_____

_____

_____

_____

Places I/We Recommend (Restaurants - Entertainment — Must See Sites)

_____

_____

_____

_____

Guest Name/s: _____

Dates of my/our visit: _____ To _____   I/we traveled from: _____

Reason for my/our trip: _____

Message to the host: _____

_____

_____

Favorite Moments / Special Highlights Of My/Our Stay

_____

_____

_____

_____

Places I/We Recommend (Restaurants - Entertainment — Must See Sites)

_____

_____

_____

_____

Guest Name/s: _____

Dates of my/our visit: _____ To _____ I/we traveled from: _____

Reason for my/our trip: _____

Message to the host: _____

_____

_____

Favorite Moments / Special Highlights Of My/Our Stay

_____

_____

_____

_____

Places I/We Recommend (Restaurants - Entertainment — Must See Sites)

_____

_____

_____

_____

Guest Name/s: _____

Dates of my/our visit: _____ To _____ I/we traveled from: _____

Reason for my/our trip: _____

Message to the host: _____

_____

_____

Favorite Moments / Special Highlights Of My/Our Stay

_____

_____

_____

_____

Places I/We Recommend (Restaurants - Entertainment – Must See Sites)

_____

_____

_____

_____

Guest Name/s: _____

Dates of my/our visit: _____ To _____ I/we traveled from: _____

Reason for my/our trip: _____

Message to the host: _____

_____

_____

Favorite Moments / Special Highlights Of My/Our Stay

_____

_____

_____

_____

Places I/We Recommend (Restaurants - Entertainment — Must See Sites)

_____

_____

_____

_____

Guest Name/s: _____

Dates of my/our visit: _____ To _____ I/we traveled from: _____

Reason for my/our trip: _____

Message to the host: _____

_____

_____

Favorite Moments / Special Highlights Of My/Our Stay

_____

_____

_____

_____

Places I/We Recommend (Restaurants - Entertainment — Must See Sites)

_____

_____

_____

_____

Guest Name/s: _____

Dates of my/our visit: _____ To _____ I/we traveled from: _____

Reason for my/our trip: _____

Message to the host: _____

_____

_____

Favorite Moments / Special Highlights Of My/Our Stay

_____

_____

_____

_____

Places I/We Recommend (Restaurants - Entertainment — Must See Sites)

_____

_____

_____

_____

Guest Name/s: _____

Dates of my/our visit: _____ To _____ I/we traveled from: _____

Reason for my/our trip: _____

Message to the host: _____
_____
_____

Favorite Moments / Special Highlights Of My/Our Stay

_____
_____
_____
_____

Places I/We Recommend (Restaurants - Entertainment — Must See Sites)

_____
_____
_____
_____

Guest Name/s: _____

Dates of my/our visit: _____ To _____ I/we traveled from: _____

Reason for my/our trip: _____

◄◄━━━━◄■►━━━━►►

Message to the host: _____
_____
_____

◄◄━━━━◄■►━━━━►►

Favorite Moments / Special Highlights Of My/Our Stay

_____
_____
_____
_____

◄◄━━━━◄■►━━━━►►

Places I/We Recommend (Restaurants - Entertainment — Must See Sites)

_____
_____
_____
_____

Guest Name/s: _____

Dates of my/our visit: _____ To _____ I/we traveled from: _____

Reason for my/our trip: _____

Message to the host: _____

_____

_____

Favorite Moments / Special Highlights Of My/Our Stay

_____

_____

_____

_____

Places I/We Recommend (Restaurants - Entertainment — Must See Sites)

_____

_____

_____

_____

Guest Name/s: _____

Dates of my/our visit: _____ To _____ I/we traveled from: _____

Reason for my/our trip: _____

Message to the host: _____
_____
_____

Favorite Moments / Special Highlights Of My/Our Stay

_____
_____
_____
_____

Places I/We Recommend (Restaurants - Entertainment — Must See Sites)

_____
_____
_____
_____

Guest Name/s: _____

Dates of my/our visit: _____ To _____ I/we traveled from: _____

Reason for my/our trip: _____

Message to the host: _____
_____
_____

Favorite Moments / Special Highlights Of My/Our Stay

_____
_____
_____
_____

Places I/We Recommend (Restaurants - Entertainment — Must See Sites)

_____
_____
_____
_____

Guest Name/s: _____

Dates of my/our visit: _____ To _____ I/we traveled from: _____

Reason for my/our trip: _____

Message to the host: _____

_____

_____

Favorite Moments / Special Highlights Of My/Our Stay

_____

_____

_____

_____

Places I/We Recommend (Restaurants - Entertainment — Must See Sites)

_____

_____

_____

_____

Guest Name/s: _____

Dates of my/our visit: _____ To _____ I/we traveled from: _____

Reason for my/our trip: _____

Message to the host: _____
_____
_____

Favorite Moments / Special Highlights Of My/Our Stay

_____
_____
_____
_____

Places I/We Recommend (Restaurants - Entertainment — Must See Sites)

_____
_____
_____
_____

Guest Name/s: _____

Dates of my/our visit: _____ To _____ I/we traveled from: _____

Reason for my/our trip: _____

Message to the host: _____

_____

_____

Favorite Moments / Special Highlights Of My/Our Stay

_____

_____

_____

_____

Places I/We Recommend (Restaurants - Entertainment — Must See Sites)

_____

_____

_____

_____

Guest Name/s: _____

Dates of my/our visit: _____ To _____ I/we traveled from: _____

Reason for my/our trip: _____

Message to the host: _____

_____

_____

Favorite Moments / Special Highlights Of My/Our Stay

_____

_____

_____

_____

Places I/We Recommend (Restaurants - Entertainment — Must See Sites)

_____

_____

_____

_____

Guest Name/s: _____

Dates of my/our visit: _____ To _____ I/we traveled from: _____

Reason for my/our trip: _____

Message to the host: _____

_____

_____

Favorite Moments / Special Highlights Of My/Our Stay

_____

_____

_____

_____

Places I/We Recommend (Restaurants - Entertainment – Must See Sites)

_____

_____

_____

_____

Guest Name/s: _____

Dates of my/our visit: _____ To _____ I/we traveled from: _____

Reason for my/our trip: _____

Message to the host: _____

_____

_____

Favorite Moments / Special Highlights Of My/Our Stay

_____

_____

_____

_____

Places I/We Recommend (Restaurants - Entertainment — Must See Sites)

_____

_____

_____

_____

Guest Name/s: _____

Dates of my/our visit: _____ To _____ I/we traveled from: _____

Reason for my/our trip: _____

Message to the host: _____

_____

_____

Favorite Moments / Special Highlights Of My/Our Stay

_____

_____

_____

_____

Places I/We Recommend (Restaurants - Entertainment — Must See Sites)

_____

_____

_____

_____

Guest Name/s: _____

Dates of my/our visit: _____ To _____ I/we traveled from: _____

Reason for my/our trip: _____

Message to the host: _____

_____

_____

Favorite Moments / Special Highlights Of My/Our Stay

_____

_____

_____

_____

Places I/We Recommend (Restaurants - Entertainment — Must See Sites)

_____

_____

_____

_____

Guest Name/s: _____

Dates of my/our visit: _____ To _____ I/we traveled from: _____

Reason for my/our trip: _____

Message to the host: _____

_____

_____

Favorite Moments / Special Highlights Of My/Our Stay

_____

_____

_____

_____

Places I/We Recommend (Restaurants - Entertainment — Must See Sites)

_____

_____

_____

_____

Guest Name/s: _____

Dates of my/our visit: _____ To _____ I/we traveled from: _____

Reason for my/our trip: _____

Message to the host: _____
_____
_____

Favorite Moments / Special Highlights Of My/Our Stay

_____
_____
_____
_____

Places I/We Recommend (Restaurants - Entertainment – Must See Sites)

_____
_____
_____
_____

Guest Name/s: _____

Dates of my/our visit: _____ To _____ I/we traveled from: _____

Reason for my/our trip: _____

Message to the host: _____
_____
_____

Favorite Moments / Special Highlights Of My/Our Stay

_____
_____
_____
_____

Places I/We Recommend (Restaurants - Entertainment — Must See Sites)

_____
_____
_____
_____

Guest Name/s: _____

Dates of my/our visit: _____ To _____ I/we traveled from: _____

Reason for my/our trip: _____

Message to the host: _____

_____

_____

Favorite Moments / Special Highlights Of My/Our Stay

_____

_____

_____

_____

Places I/We Recommend (Restaurants - Entertainment – Must See Sites)

_____

_____

_____

_____

Guest Name/s: _____

Dates of my/our visit: _____ To _____ I/we traveled from: _____

Reason for my/our trip: _____

Message to the host: _____

_____

_____

Favorite Moments / Special Highlights Of My/Our Stay

_____

_____

_____

_____

Places I/We Recommend (Restaurants - Entertainment — Must See Sites)

_____

_____

_____

_____

Guest Name/s: _____

Dates of my/our visit: _____ To _____ I/we traveled from: _____

Reason for my/our trip: _____

Message to the host: _____

_____

_____

_____

Favorite Moments / Special Highlights Of My/Our Stay

_____

_____

_____

_____

Places I/We Recommend (Restaurants - Entertainment – Must See Sites)

_____

_____

_____

_____

Guest Name/s: _____

Dates of my/our visit: _____ To _____   I/we traveled from: _____

Reason for my/our trip: _____

Message to the host: _____

_____

_____

Favorite Moments / Special Highlights Of My/Our Stay

_____

_____

_____

_____

Places I/We Recommend (Restaurants - Entertainment — Must See Sites)

_____

_____

_____

_____

Guest Name/s: _____

Dates of my/our visit: _____ To _____ I/we traveled from: _____

Reason for my/our trip: _____

Message to the host: _____

_____

_____

_____

Favorite Moments / Special Highlights Of My/Our Stay

_____

_____

_____

_____

_____

Places I/We Recommend (Restaurants - Entertainment – Must See Sites)

_____

_____

_____

_____

_____

Guest Name/s: _____

Dates of my/our visit: _____ To _____ I/we traveled from: _____

Reason for my/our trip: _____

Message to the host: _____

_____

_____

Favorite Moments / Special Highlights Of My/Our Stay

_____

_____

_____

_____

Places I/We Recommend (Restaurants - Entertainment — Must See Sites)

_____

_____

_____

_____

Guest Name/s: _____

Dates of my/our visit: _____ To _____ I/we traveled from: _____

Reason for my/our trip: _____

Message to the host: _____
_____
_____
_____

Favorite Moments / Special Highlights Of My/Our Stay

_____
_____
_____
_____

Places I/We Recommend (Restaurants - Entertainment — Must See Sites)

_____
_____
_____
_____

Guest Name/s: _____

Dates of my/our visit: _____ To _____ I/we traveled from: _____

Reason for my/our trip: _____

Message to the host: _____

_____

_____

Favorite Moments / Special Highlights Of My/Our Stay

_____

_____

_____

_____

Places I/We Recommend (Restaurants - Entertainment — Must See Sites)

_____

_____

_____

_____

Guest Name/s: _____

Dates of my/our visit: _____ To _____ I/we traveled from: _____

Reason for my/our trip: _____

Message to the host: _____
_____
_____

Favorite Moments / Special Highlights Of My/Our Stay

_____
_____
_____
_____

Places I/We Recommend (Restaurants - Entertainment — Must See Sites)

_____
_____
_____
_____

Made in the USA
Las Vegas, NV
15 October 2022

57359915R00063